FACT CAT

THE EARTH

Alice Harman

WAYLAND

FACT CAT

Get your paws on this fantastic new mega-series from Wayland!

Join our Fact Cat on a journey of fun learning about every subject under the sun!

First published in paperback in 2015 by Wayland
© Wayland 2015

All rights reserved.
Dewey Number: 525-dc23
ISBN: 978 0 7502 8892 7
Library eBook ISBN: 978 0 7502 8522 3

MIX
Paper from responsible sources
FSC® C104740

Produced for Wayland by
White-Thomson Publishing Ltd
www.wtpub.co.uk
+44 (0) 843 208 7460

10 9 8 7 6 5 4 3 2 1

Editor: Alice Harman
Design: Rocket Design (East Anglia) Ltd
Fact Cat illustrations: Shutterstock/Julien Troneur
Other illustrations: Stefan Chabluk/Bill Donohue
Consultant: Kate Ruttle

A catalogue for this title is available from the British Library

Wayland, an imprint of Hachette Children's Group
Part of Hodder & Stoughton
Carmelite House
50 Victoria Embankment
London EC4Y 0DZ

An Hachette UK company.
www.hachette.co.uk
www.hachettechildrens.co.uk

Printed and bound in China

Picture and illustration credits:
Chabluk, Stefan: 18; Donohoe, William: 4-5;
Dreamstime: Sebastian Kaulitzki 6 (t), Psdphotography 11, Tiero 13, Yasushitanikado 14, Mesquite53 17, Lakeside 20, Wimclaes 20; NASA: 10, title page, cover, 21;
Shutterstock: Alberto Loyo 6 (b), vaida 7 inset, Mopic 8, Ammit Jack 9, BlueRingMedia 12, S. Borisov 15, Ingrid Prats 19; Wiki Commons Justin1569 16.

Every effort has been made to clear copyright. Should there be any inadvertent omission, please apply to the publisher for rectification.

FACT CAT FACT

There is a question for you to answer on each spread in this book. You can check your answers on page 24.

CONTENTS

EARTH IN SPACE

Earth is one of eight **planets** that move around a **star** called the Sun. This star gives out heat and light. Earth is the third closest planet to the Sun.

Six of the planets have moons. Moons are made of rock or ice, and they move around a planet. In what year did humans first land on Earth's moon?

Saturn

Uranus

Neptune

FACT CAT FACT

Venus moves closer to Earth than any other planet. After the Sun and the Moon, it is the brightest object you can see in the sky.

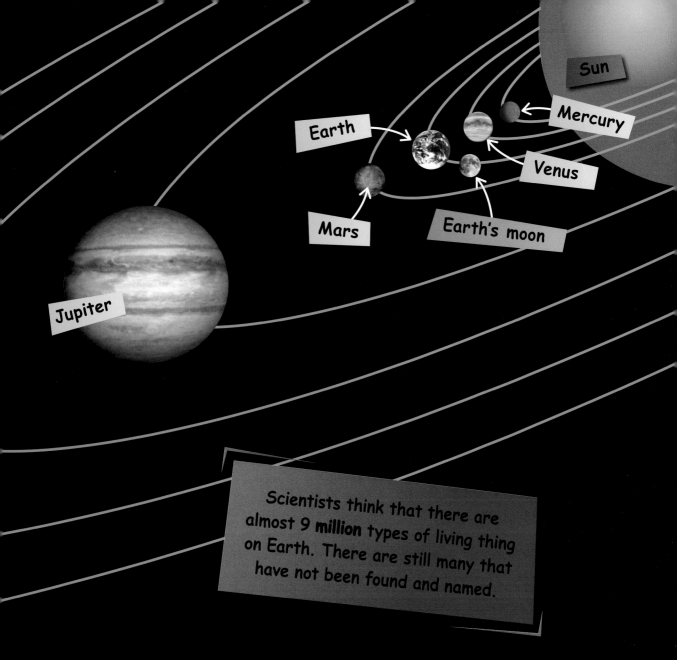

Sun

Mercury

Earth

Venus

Mars

Earth's moon

Jupiter

Scientists think that there are almost 9 **million** types of living thing on Earth. There are still many that have not been found and named.

All the other planets around the Sun are too hot or too cold for anything to live on them. Earth is the only planet that has plants, animals and other living things.

EARTH'S HISTORY

The way that living things develop over time is called **evolution**. Can you find out which scientist first wrote about evolution?

Earth is more than 4 **billion** years old. The first living things were tiny, simple creatures called bacteria. Over billions of years, they changed into bigger, more **complex** creatures such as **jellyfish**.

bacteria (as seen under a **microscope**)

jellyfish

FACT CAT FACT

Humans didn't exist until 200,000 years ago. If you imagine the Earth is ten years old, it's as if humans have been around for less than four hours.

Dinosaurs first lived on Earth about 220 million years ago. There were at least 1000 different types of dinosaur. They all died out around 65 million years ago, and scientists still aren't sure why.

We know that dinosaurs existed because people have found their **skeletons** deep underground.

INSIDE THE EARTH

Most of Earth is made of rock. Earth's thin **surface** layer is called the **crust**. Underneath the **solid** crust, the rock is so hot that it partly turns to **liquid**. This layer is called the **mantle**.

mantle

outer core

crust

inner core

Earth has a **core** of **metal** at its centre. Try to find out which scientists think is hotter – the centre of Earth or the surface of the Sun.

Earth's crust is made of huge pieces of rock. They float around slowly on the mantle below. When they crash into each other, they can form mountains or **volcanoes** and cause **earthquakes**.

A volcano is a rocky hill that has built up around an opening in the Earth's crust. When a volcano erupts, liquid rock comes up on to Earth's surface.

FACT CAT FACT

Most of Earth's volcanoes are found in one area around the Pacific Ocean. It is called the Pacific Ring of Fire. Almost all earthquakes take place here, too.

WATER

Most of the Earth's surface is covered in water. The oceans contain almost all of this water. Ocean water is salty, and fresh water is not. Humans have still only explored a tiny area of the oceans.

FACT CAT FACT

The Mariana Trench is the deepest part of the ocean. If someone stood at the bottom of the trench, the weight of the water on top of them would be as heavy as fifty large aeroplanes.

What animals can you think of that live in the oceans? Try to make a list of five animals.

Earth is getting hotter, and some of its ice is **melting**. This means there is extra water in the oceans. If the oceans get too full, they will **flood** the land.

LAND

Earth has seven large areas of land. These are called **continents**. Each continent is **surrounded** by water. However, until 200 million years ago all these continents were joined together.

Europe

Asia

North America

Africa

South America

Antarctica

Australia

This map shows Earth's continents as they are today. Do you know which continent is the only one where people do not live?

Earth has many different types of **environment**, such as desert, jungle, grassland and mountains. The coldest, driest parts of Earth are at its top and bottom. The hottest, wettest areas are around its centre.

The rainforest is a type of hot, wet forest where plants grow very well. Over half of all types of life are found in Earth's rainforests.

FACT CAT FACT

People cut down the rainforest for wood and to make space for farms. If they continue doing this at the same speed as today, all of Earth's rainforest will be gone by 2060.

EARTH'S ATMOSPHERE

Earth's atmosphere is a thin layer of gases that surrounds the planet. Life on Earth could not exist without this atmosphere. It stops Earth getting too hot or cold.

The Northern and Southern Lights appear in the night sky when **rays** from the Sun hit the outer layer of Earth's atmosphere. Find out in which countries you can see the Northern Lights.

FACT CAT FACT

The Earth's atmosphere protects it from objects travelling very fast through space. Huge chunks of rock and metal slow down a lot when they enter the atmosphere. This makes them burn up into very small parts.

The inner layer of Earth's atmosphere contains air. This is a mixture of gases that includes nitrogen, oxygen and **carbon dioxide**. Almost all animals need oxygen to survive, and almost all plants need carbon dioxide.

Cars and factories produce lots of carbon dioxide. We need many trees to take in this carbon dioxide so there is not too much of it in the atmosphere.

WEATHER

Weather is what we call changes in temperature, wind and rain. Sometimes we have **extreme** weather that is much hotter, colder, windier or wetter than usual.

Tornadoes are tubes of air that spin around very quickly and touch the ground. Find out which country has the most tornadoes.

FACT CAT FACT

At any one time, there are 1800 **storms** taking place in Earth's atmosphere.

Clouds are made of tiny drops of water and ice. These join together with other drops and become larger and heavier. When they are very heavy, they fall to the ground as rain or snow.

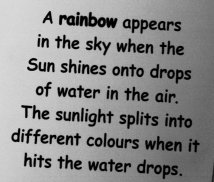

A **rainbow** appears in the sky when the Sun shines onto drops of water in the air. The sunlight splits into different colours when it hits the water drops.

DAYS AND SEASONS

When an area of Earth faces the Sun, it is day there. When an area is turned away from the Sun, it is night there.

The Earth spins once every 24 hours as it moves around the Sun. The Sun can only shine light on the part of the Earth that faces it. The other part of the Earth is dark.

day

night

Sun

Earth

light

The Earth takes one year to move all the way around the Sun. When a part of the Earth is closest to the Sun, it is summer there. When it is furthest away, it is winter there.

There are four **seasons** on Earth. They are spring, summer, autumn and winter. Which picture do you think shows which season? Why?

FACT CAT FACT

The United Kingdom and Australia are on opposite sides of Earth. At Christmas, it is winter in the United Kingdom and summer in Australia.

LIFE ON EARTH

Over time, living things change to survive better where they live. Desert animals need to stay cool and not use much water, so they have special features that allow them to do this.

A cactus stores water inside itself. A desert fox loses lots of heat from its big ears. Try to find out what special features help a **camel** live in the desert.

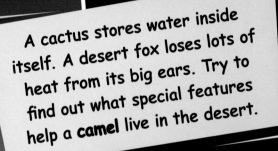

cactus

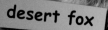

desert fox

The way that humans live has changed a lot over the last few hundred years. More than half the people on Earth now live in cities and towns rather than the countryside.

At night, the glow from city lights on Earth can be seen from space.

FACT CAT FACT

Shanghai, in China, is the largest city on Earth. More than 23 million people live there.

QUIZ

Try to answer the questions below. Look back through the book to help you. Check your answers on page 24.

1 Where is most of Earth's water?

a)   in the oceans
b)   in lakes
c)   deep underground

2 How many continents are there on Earth today?

a)   two
b)   five
c)   seven

3 Almost all animals on Earth need oxygen to survive. True or not true?

a)   true
b)   not true

4 What is Earth's core made of?

a)   rock
b)   metal
c)   wood

5 Were dinosaurs and humans ever alive on Earth at the same time?

a)   yes
b)   no

6 How many seasons are there on Earth?

a)   four
b)   nine
c)   five

GLOSSARY

billion a thousand million (1,000,000,000)

camel big animal with one or two humps on its back

carbon dioxide a gas that contains carbon and oxygen

complex opposite of simple

continent one of seven very large areas of land in the world; Europe is one of the continents

core part at the centre of the Earth

crust outside layer of the Earth

dinosaur animal like a huge lizard that lived millions of years ago

earthquake sudden, strong shaking of the ground

environment the world we live in, especially the plants, animals and things around us

evolution how living things change over time

extreme stronger or more fierce than normal

flood when a lot of water spreads over the land

jellyfish sea animal that has a soft, clear body

liquid form of material that can flow and that is wet, like water

mantle hot, partly liquid layer below Earth's crust

melt when something solid turns to liquid because it has become warm

metal material that is normally hard and shiny, like gold

microscope instrument that makes tiny things look bigger

million a thousand thousands (1,000,000)

planet large object in space that moves around a star

rainbow curved band of different colours you see in the sky when the Sun shines through rain

ray beam of light or heat

seasons the four seasons are the four parts of the year, which are spring, summer, autumn and winter

skeleton all the bones that are in a body

solid form of material that you can normally see and touch, like rock

star large object in space that is made of burning gases

storm strong wind and rain or snow

surface top layer of an object

surrounded when an object has something forming a circle all, or nearly all, the way around it

tornado very strong wind that forms a tall tube shape

volcano hill with a hole in its centre that liquid rock can come up through from deep underground

INDEX

ANSWERS

Pages 4-20

page 4: 1969

page 6: Charles Darwin

page 8: the centre of Earth

page 10: The Great Barrier Reef, which is off the coast of Australia

page 12: Antarctica

page 14: Canada, Iceland, Greenland, Norway, Sweden, Finland, Alaska (part of the USA), Russia and sometimes Scotland (part of the UK)

page 16: The USA - it usually has more than 1000 every year.

page 19: Top left - spring; top right - summer; bottom left - autumn; bottom right - winter

page 20: Their special features include: long eyelashes to keep sand out of their eyes; wide feet so they don't sink into the sand; a hump of fat to store energy so they can stay alive without food for a long time.

Quiz answers

1   a) in the oceans
2   c) seven
3   a) true
4   b) metal
5   b) no
6   a) four